GET INFORMED—STAY INFORMED

GUN
VIOLENCE

Natalie Hyde

CRABTREE
PUBLISHING COMPANY
WWW.CRABTREEBOOKS.COM

Author: Natalie Hyde
Series research and development:
    Reagan Miller
Editor-in-chief: Lionel Bender
Editor: Ellen Rodger
Proofreaders: Laura Booth,
    Melissa Boyce
Project coordinator: Petrice Custance
Design and photo research:
    Ben White
Production: Kim Richardson
**Production coordinator and
    Prepress technician:** Tammy McGarr
Print coordinator: Katherine Berti
Consultant: Emily Drew,
    The New York Public Library

Produced for Crabtree
Publishing Company by
Bender Richardson White

Photographs and reproductions: Alamy: 7 (Storms Media Group), 8–9 (Richard Levine), 17 (Gregory Perkins), 18–19 (CBW), 20–21 (Mario Beauregard Beaustock), 22–23 (Arterra Picture Library), 30–31 (RosaIreneBetancourt13), 32–33 (David Nelson); Getty Images: 10 (Dirck Halstead), 10 (Godong/UIG), 16–17 (Usman Khan/AFP), 17 (RichLegg), 26–27 (Miami Herald), 29 (Kent Betancur), 34–35 (Laura Buckman/Bloomberg), 36 (Loren Elliott), 39 (China News Service); Shutterstock: 1 (bakdc), 4–5 (evenfh), 6–7 (Rob Crandall), 9 (Florida Chuck), 12–13 (Harry Thomas Flower), 14–15 (DmyTo), 19 (Louis.Roth), 24–25 (RoidRanger), 27 (Brent Eysler), 28–29 (Spill Photography), 33 (ja–images), 35 (Scott Cornell), 37 (Roy Harris), 38 (PRESSLAB), 40–41 (Linda Moon), 42–43 (Monkey Business Images); Icons

Diagrams: Stefan Chabluk, using the following as sources of data: p. 7 www.bradycampaign.org, p. 13 United Nations Small Arms Survey and Ted Miller, Pacific Institute for Research and Evaluation, p. 22 Centers for Disease Control and Prevention/Vox.com, p. 26 Pew Research Center, p. 28 Pew Research Center, p. 37 Statistics Canada/rawnumbers.com, p. 38 FBI, UK Home Office, Statistics Canada, Australia Crime Statistics, p. 43 Center for Responsive Politics/NRA

Library and Archives Canada Cataloguing in Publication

Hyde, Natalie, 1963-, author
    Gun violence / Natalie Hyde.

(Get informed -- stay informed)
Includes bibliographical references and index.
Issued in print and electronic formats.
ISBN 978-0-7787-5332-2 (hardcover).--
ISBN 978-0-7787-5346-9 (softcover).--
ISBN 978-1-4271-2193-6 (HTML)

    1. Gun control--Juvenile literature. 2. Firearms and
crime--Juvenile literature. 3. Violent crimes--Prevention--
Juvenile literature. I. Title.

HV7435.H93 2019   j363.33   C2018-905648-7
                                          C2018-905649-5

Library of Congress Cataloging-in-Publication Data

Names: Hyde, Natalie, 1963- author.
Title: Gun violence / Natalie Hyde.
Description: New York : Crabtree Publishing, [2019] |
    Series: Get informed--stay inform |
    Includes bibliographical references and index.
Identifiers: LCCN 2018057989 (print) | LCCN 2019000199 (ebook) |
    ISBN 9781427121936 (Electronic) |
    ISBN 9780778753322 (hardcover : alk. paper) |
    ISBN 9780778753469 (pbk. : alk. paper)
Subjects: LCSH: Firearms and crime--United States--Juvenile
    literature. | Mass shootings--United States--Juvenile literature. |
    Gun control--United States--Juvenile literature.
Classification: LCC HV7436 (ebook) |
    LCC HV7436 .H93 2019 (print) | DDC 364.2--dc23
LC record available at https://lccn.loc.gov/2018057989

Crabtree Publishing Company
www.crabtreebooks.com   1-800-387-7650

Printed in the U.S.A./032019/CG20190118

Published in Canada
Crabtree Publishing
616 Welland Ave.
St. Catharines, ON
L2M 5V6

Published in the United States
Crabtree Publishing
PMB 59051
350 Fifth Avenue, 59th Floor
New York, NY 10118

Published in the United Kingdom
Crabtree Publishing
Maritime House
Basin Road North, Hove
BN41 1WR

Published in Australia
Crabtree Publishing
Unit 3 – 5 Currumbin Court
Capalaba
QLD 4157

CONTENTS

Every single day, there is a mass shooting somewhere in the United States. A mass shooting is usually defined as an event where four or more people are injured or killed by **firearms**. There are more mass shootings in the United States than in any other country in the world. They have become so common that they often don't make the news beyond local newpapers and TV and radio stations.

▼ A memorial was created after the October 1, 2017 mass shooting in Las Vegas, where 58 people were killed and hundreds were wounded by one gunman.

"We lose eight children and teenagers to gun violence every day. If a mysterious virus suddenly started killing eight of our children every day, America would **mobilize** teams of doctors and public health officials. We would move heaven and Earth until we found a way to protect our children. But not with gun violence."

Elizabeth Warren, politician and senator of Massachusetts

QUESTIONS TO ASK

Within this book are three types of boxes with questions to help your critical thinking about gun violence. The icons will help you identify them.

THE CENTRAL ISSUES
Learning about the main points of information.

WHAT'S AT STAKE
Helping you determine how the issue will affect you.

ASK YOUR OWN QUESTIONS
Prompts to address gaps in your understanding.

STUDENTS UNDER FIRE

Mass shootings in schools are becoming frequent too. There are 57 times more school shootings in the United States than in any other nation. That means the number of students who have experienced shooting during school hours is higher than the populations of many towns. People around the world recognize the names Columbine, Virginia Tech, Sandy Hook, and Marjory Stoneman Douglas because of the **tragedy** of gun violence that occurred in those schools.

AFFECTING EVERYONE

Beyond mass shootings, all gun violence is on the rise in both the United States and Canada. In some major Canadian cities, the number of gun crimes has almost doubled over the past five years. At least half of gun deaths are related to gang activity. Canada has less strict gun laws than the United Kingdom, Japan, or Australia, and more gun violence. Many guns are illegally **smuggled** across the border from the United States.

What has caused this changing landscape of gun violence? Is there anything citizens can do to lower the number of shootings? These are the questions you may be asking yourself. Gun violence can be a frightening and divisive topic, but it is something that affects almost everyone. You probably know friends, family, or neighbors whose lives have been changed because of it. Understanding how the issue is changing and what can be done to lessen gun violence means doing research and seeing different points of view.

Getting informed about where gun violence is happening, why it is increasing, and how it affects people's lives is important. It will help you protect yourself, lessen your risk, and help you make changes in **society** that will hopefully reduce gun violence. To do this, you need to find accurate information and **analyze** it carefully.

If you don't have knowledge and understanding of a topic, you may be **swayed** by support groups and organizations that do not have your health and safety in mind. If you aren't aware of how laws are created or changed, you might find your rights and **privileges** can be taken away more easily. You may make bad decisions when you vote for **politicians** who are supposed to represent you.

WHO CAN YOU TRUST?

Nobody wants gun violence, but there is a lot of **debate** on how it should be dealt with. Some people believe that gun violence is inescapable in our society. They want to continue to own and carry guns to protect themselves and their families. Others believe that gun violence is the result of more guns in **communities**, and the fact that they are too easy to access. As you begin your search for information, you will notice that the facts will support one side or the other. Strong **lobby groups** for either side may use your fears and **prejudices** to promote their stand.

You can build your knowledge by starting with how a topic first developed and in what **context**, or setting. The context for gun violence is a time when crime and threats seem to be on the rise. Gun ownership is also rising. **Statistics** also show that every day, 96 Americans are killed with guns and approximately three million American children witness gun violence every year.

THE CENTRAL ISSUES

Do all **action groups** or organizations want you to be an informed citizen? Why might they want to keep you confused and not interested in topics like gun ownership or gun control?

▲ "March for Our Lives" protests in the United States were rallies in support of tighter gun control. They were led by high school students who had survived a mass shooting at their school.

GUN OWNERSHIP IN THE UNITED STATES, BY STATE

- 5.2–19.5%
- 19.6–34.9%
- 35.0–53.9%
- 54.0–62.8%

Based on nationwide survey of gun ownership among households, 2016

▼ Students meet with U.S. President Donald Trump at a listening session to voice their concerns over gun violence in their schools.

When you want to get informed on a topic, where do you begin? To understand what is happening now, it is always a good idea to go back and find out how, where, and why it began. It is important to identify **key** background information and key players. When researching gun violence, you can read about gun laws through history. Why were the laws created? How have they changed? Which groups want stricter gun laws? Which want fewer laws?

▶ The day after the mass shooting at Marjory Stoneman Douglas High School, the front pages of newspapers show the shock and sadness felt by students, parents, and teachers.

Students embrace after being released from a lockdown at Marjory Stoneman Douglas High School in Parkland, Florida.

The New York Times

NEW YORK, THURSDAY, FEBRUARY 15, 2018

Late Edition

Today, morning clouds, then sunshine, a mild afternoon, high 63. Tonight, periodic rain late, low 53. Tomorrow, a few morning showers, high 58. Weather map, Page B8.

$3.00

ORROR AT FLORIDA SCHOOL; EX-STUDENT HELD

At Least 17 Die

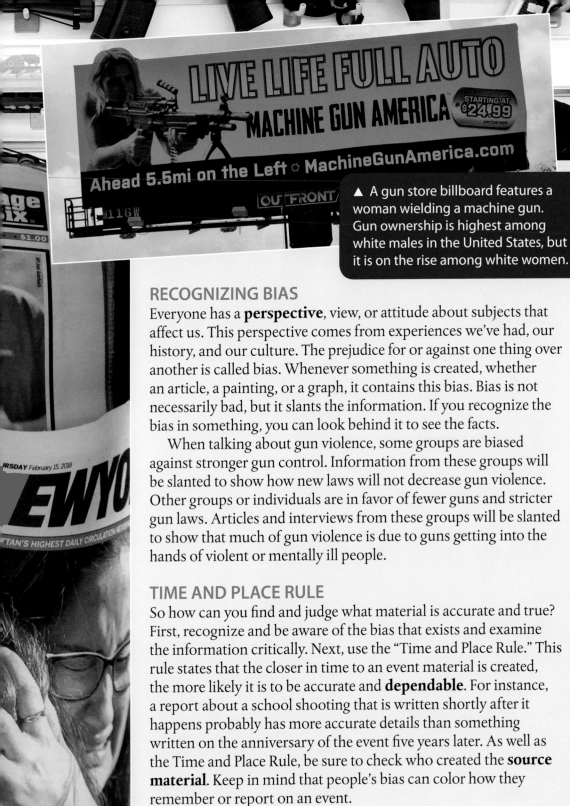

▲ A gun store billboard features a woman wielding a machine gun. Gun ownership is highest among white males in the United States, but it is on the rise among white women.

RECOGNIZING BIAS

Everyone has a **perspective**, view, or attitude about subjects that affect us. This perspective comes from experiences we've had, our history, and our culture. The prejudice for or against one thing over another is called bias. Whenever something is created, whether an article, a painting, or a graph, it contains this bias. Bias is not necessarily bad, but it slants the information. If you recognize the bias in something, you can look behind it to see the facts.

When talking about gun violence, some groups are biased against stronger gun control. Information from these groups will be slanted to show how new laws will not decrease gun violence. Other groups or individuals are in favor of fewer guns and stricter gun laws. Articles and interviews from these groups will be slanted to show that much of gun violence is due to guns getting into the hands of violent or mentally ill people.

TIME AND PLACE RULE

So how can you find and judge what material is accurate and true? First, recognize and be aware of the bias that exists and examine the information critically. Next, use the "Time and Place Rule." This rule states that the closer in time to an event material is created, the more likely it is to be accurate and **dependable**. For instance, a report about a school shooting that is written shortly after it happens probably has more accurate details than something written on the anniversary of the event five years later. As well as the Time and Place Rule, be sure to check who created the **source material**. Keep in mind that people's bias can color how they remember or report on an event.

▲ Although he survived being shot, Brady's death 33 years later was ruled by the medical examiner as a homicide caused by the gunshot in 1981.

In 1981, White House Press Secretary **James Brady** was shot by a mentally ill person who was trying to **assassinate** U.S. President Ronald Reagan. Disabled by the injury to his brain, he and his wife Sarah founded the Brady Campaign to Prevent Gun Violence. Its **mission** is to cut gun deaths in half in America by the year 2025.

◀ Some people blame increased gun violence on video games. However, there have been no reliable studies that find a link between children playing these games and increased violent behavior.

KEY INFORMATION

Primary sources are firsthand evidence of a topic, made by the people involved in or who witnessed the events. A police report of a mass shooting is one example.
Secondary sources are reports, analyses, and **interpretations** of the primary sources, such as statistics collected from several different sources on gun **homicides**.
Tertiary sources are summaries or **databases** of primary and secondary information. They include things such as Wikipedia articles or entries in encyclopedias.

Evidence about a topic is called source material. It can be things you read, such as reports or newspaper articles. It can be things you look at, such as maps, charts, and photographs. It can also be things you hear or touch, such as recorded interviews or posters from protest marches. Source material can be found in many places, including libraries, museums, and online.

WHERE TO LOOK AND LISTEN

Some sources of information you can check are:
- newspapers—local and national press
- television—broadcast, cable, and satellite
- blogs, diaries, and personal interviews
- Facebook pages
- Twitter feed
- Snapchat and Pinterest
- government reports
- textbooks and classroom resources
- magazines and journals
- radio programs and podcasts
- Google Alerts

Also check online news outlets for young people such as:
- *TIME for Kids*
- *The Washington Post KidsPost*
- *CBC Kids* (Canadian Broadcasting Corporation)

When researching and collecting source material on gun violence you will be able to understand what has happened on the topic to date. You will be able to see the different sides of the subject and learn how historians, who study the past, have considered it. It will help you see where things stand today and who is affected by gun violence.

> *But we are smart enough, compassionate enough, to balance legitimate Second Amendment rights with preventive measures.*
>
> Hillary Clinton, U.S. politician and diplomat

In order to understand a topic, you must learn its key vocabulary, terms, and concepts. For example, gun violence articles and reports will often refer to lobby groups—people strongly supporting a particular cause; licenses—permits to do something; and different types of guns such as assault rifles (a rapid-fire gun), shotguns (fire small shot), and AR-15s (semiautomatic rifles). As you research, you will discover new terms to learn.

A reliable dictionary, either in print or online, is a good place to start. Asking other people what they think a word means or what a group stands for, might include their bias. Dictionaries give **objective** definitions. Knowing key terms will help you read material accurately.

ASK YOUR OWN QUESTIONS

To determine if a source is **credible**, consider:
- Does the creator have solid credentials and expertise in the topic?
- Does the headline match the story?
- Is the publisher known to be reliable?
- What sources did the creator use?
- Is the source relevant and up to date?
- Is the source meant to be a joke or **clickbait**?

GUN-RELATED DEATHS PER MILLION OF POPULATION
Homicides by firearm per one million people

Australia	1.4
New Zealand	1.6
Germany	1.9
Austria	2.2
Denmark	2.7
Netherlands	3.2
Sweden	4.1
Finland	4.5
Ireland	4.8
Canada	5.1
Luxembourg	6.2
Belgium	6.8
Switzerland	7.7
United States	29.7

Based on national figures for all countries for 2012–2014

PRICE TO U.S. SOCIETY OF A MURDER
Includes costs to public services and the victim's family

TOTAL $441,000

Murderer's prison costs: $414,000

Policework: $2,200
Emergency services: $450
Victim's hospital costs: $10,700
Victim's family support: $11,600
Murderer's court costs: $2,300

Charts, graphs, and maps are a visual way to gain information about a topic. When reading charts and graphs, check to see who **compiled** the data. This will help you identify the bias. The websites for Statistics Canada and the U.S. Census Bureau are good places to start. They offer national data on a wide variety of subjects. They have high standards for collecting and sorting data and their aim is to be unbiased.

◄ The annual U.S. National Rifle Association of America (NRA) convention draws more than 80,000 people to gun exhibits, seminars, and workshops. The NRA is a nonprofit **civil rights** organization and lobby group with almost five million members.

MAKING SENSE OF STATISTICS
Gun violence is a large problem affecting many people all over the world. Visual information, such as graphs, charts, and maps, is often useful to help narrow your focus to one region or one segment of society. It can help you comprehend the relationship between numbers or better understand how things are changing. You can see if gun violence is increasing and where. Graphs can help you determine if new laws are reducing violence or not.

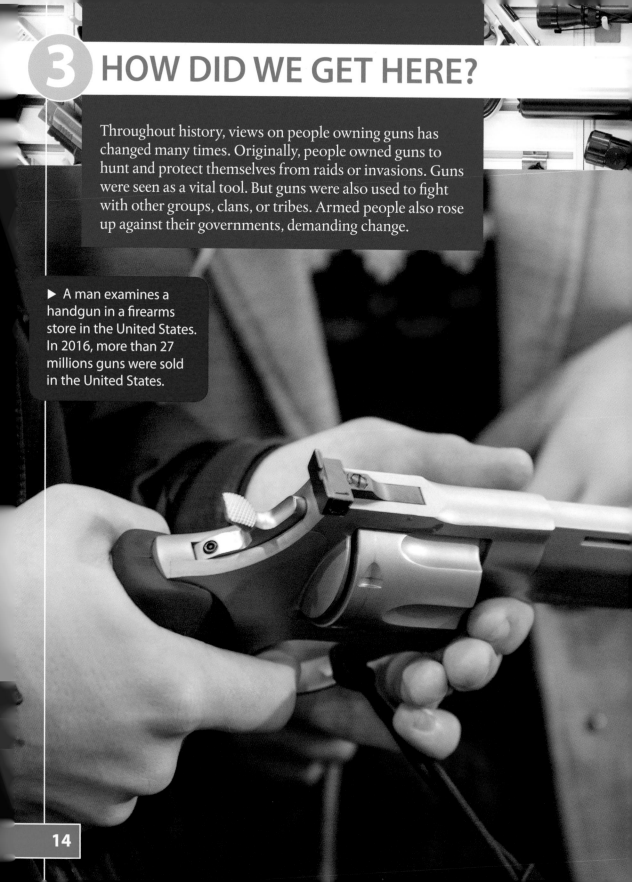

Throughout history, views on people owning guns has changed many times. Originally, people owned guns to hunt and protect themselves from raids or invasions. Guns were seen as a vital tool. But guns were also used to fight with other groups, clans, or tribes. Armed people also rose up against their governments, demanding change.

▶ A man examines a handgun in a firearms store in the United States. In 2016, more than 27 millions guns were sold in the United States.

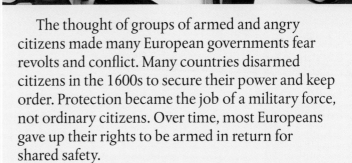

America is a country founded on guns. It's in our DNA. It's very strange but I feel better having a gun.

U.S. actor Brad Pitt

The thought of groups of armed and angry citizens made many European governments fear revolts and conflict. Many countries disarmed citizens in the 1600s to secure their power and keep order. Protection became the job of a military force, not ordinary citizens. Over time, most Europeans gave up their rights to be armed in return for shared safety.

PROTECTING A FREE STATE

In Colonial America (1607–1763) all able-bodied men from the ages of 18 to 45 were required to be part of a militia. These armed groups were established to protect the new colonies from outside threats. In 1773, when colonists threatened to revolt over British rule, Britain attempted to gain control by disarming them. This led to the first battles of the American Revolutionary War (1775–1783) in Lexington and Concord, Massachusetts.

After the war, when independence was gained, the founding fathers were determined to support a militia and its right to bear arms. They wanted to make sure they would always be able to support the people if a government was **corrupt**. In 1791, they included the Second Amendment in the U.S. Constitution (see Key Facts panel).

For many U.S. citizens, the Second Amendment means that private gun ownership is their right. Any attempt at regulation or control over how many or what type of guns should be allowed is considered a **violation** of that right. Gun ownership is tied into the history of the country. Constitutional experts have continually interpreted the meaning of the right to bear arms both historically and in today's society.

Following negotiations between Britain and its remaining North American colonies, Canada was formed in 1867. The country's constitution at the time—the British North America Act—said nothing about gun rights. Before 1892 and the first Criminal Code, hunting rifles were common but people could be jailed for carrying a handgun unless they could prove they were in danger of being attacked. Today, Canadian law requires everyone owning a gun to have a license. Getting a license includes a **background check**, safety training, and a waiting period of 28 days. Canadian gun laws are more restrictive than American gun laws, but weaker than the gun laws of many European countries.

During World War II (1939–1945), all Canadian citizens had to register their guns. This was stopped after the war, but handguns still had to be registered. After a mass shooting at the École Polytechnique in Montreal in 1989, where 14 women were killed, a new gun **registry** was started. In 2012, that

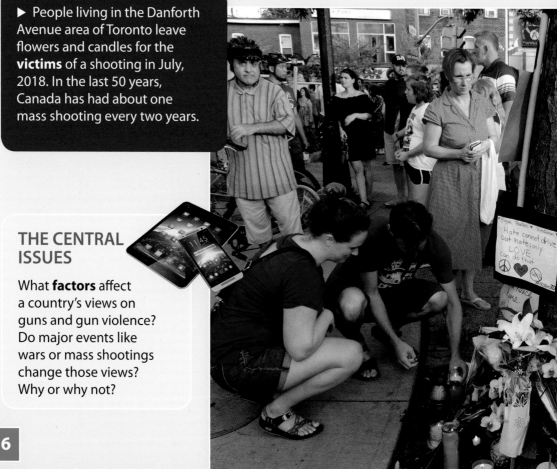

▶ People living in the Danforth Avenue area of Toronto leave flowers and candles for the **victims** of a shooting in July, 2018. In the last 50 years, Canada has had about one mass shooting every two years.

THE CENTRAL ISSUES

What **factors** affect a country's views on guns and gun violence? Do major events like wars or mass shootings change those views? Why or why not?

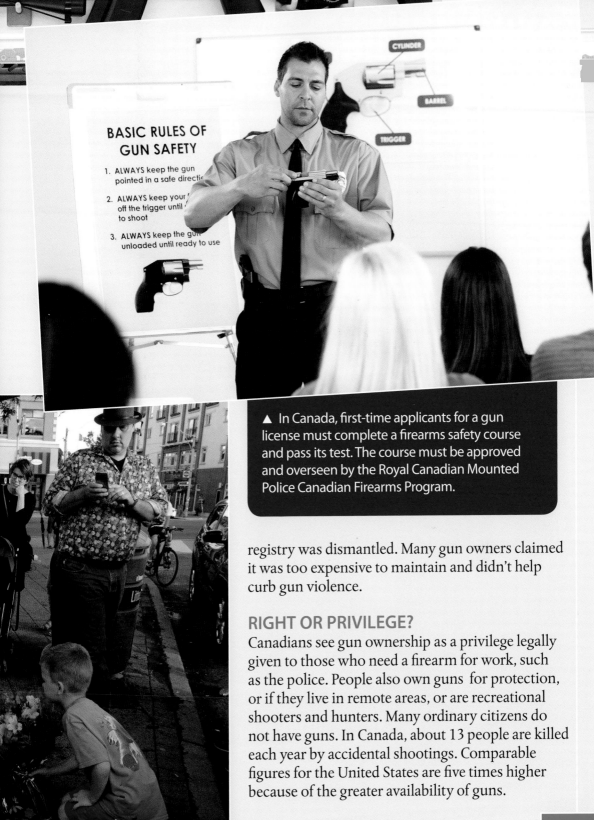

BASIC RULES OF
GUN SAFETY

1. ALWAYS keep the gun
   pointed in a safe directi...

2. ALWAYS keep your ...
   off the trigger until ...
   to shoot

3. ALWAYS keep the gu...
   unloaded until ready to use

CYLINDER

BARREL

TRIGGER

▲ In Canada, first-time applicants for a gun license must complete a firearms safety course and pass its test. The course must be approved and overseen by the Royal Canadian Mounted Police Canadian Firearms Program.

registry was dismantled. Many gun owners claimed it was too expensive to maintain and didn't help curb gun violence.

RIGHT OR PRIVILEGE?

Canadians see gun ownership as a privilege legally given to those who need a firearm for work, such as the police. People also own guns for protection, or if they live in remote areas, or are recreational shooters and hunters. Many ordinary citizens do not have guns. In Canada, about 13 people are killed each year by accidental shootings. Comparable figures for the United States are five times higher because of the greater availability of guns.

Gun violence includes single shootings as well as mass shootings. Overall, mass shootings get the most attention. They are shocking and emotionally charged and the **media** gives a lot of coverage to these events. Because they are shocking, they focus people's attention on gun violence. They are cited for changing people's attitudes toward gun violence and, in some cases, changing laws on gun violence.

Mass shootings have changed over time. According to Global Research, from the 1920s to

> " *The stronger our gun control laws are, the fewer acts of violence including mass violence that will happen in our society.* "
>
> Senator Joseph Lieberman of Connecticut in an interview after the Sandy Hook massacre, 2012

▶ The Las Vegas mass shooting in 2017 killed 58 people and injured about 800 more. The shooter used a "bump stock" on a semiautomatic gun, making it fully automatic. From a room high up in a hotel he fired on a crowd for more than 15 minutes. The U.S. government is considering banning all bump stocks.

Protesters at a 2018 "March for Our Lives" rally in Toronto, Canada, call for gun law reform. Rallies bring attention to an issue, but are not always successful at getting laws changed.

the 1960s they tended to be among families or the result of **criminals** trying to escape the law. In recent years, targets are often random strangers and the shootings are in public places.

TIME FOR A CHANGE

Mass shootings bring the issue of gun violence into sharp focus and make people want to push for gun control. In 1996, there was a key event in Port Arthur, Tasmania. Thirty-five people were killed and 23 were wounded. The shooting led to new gun laws in Australia. Certain weapons were banned. New rules for gun licenses were also created. There have been no mass shootings in Australia since then.

In the United States, the Columbine High School shooting in 1999 made a lasting mark on society. It was the worst shooting by children against children. Two senior students at the school killed 12 students and one teacher and wounded more than 20 others. It sparked debates on gun control, gun violence, bullying, and video game violence. However, no gun laws were changed. Since the Columbine shooting, there have been hundreds of school shootings, including Sandy Hook Elementary School where 26 elementary students and teachers were killed in 2012.

KEY PLAYERS

Everytown for Gun Safety is a group that works to make U.S. communities safe from gun violence. It was formed when a group of politicians met with mothers concerned about gun violence. Everytown pushes for background checks on all gun purchases. The group believes tighter permit rules can prevent violent people from buying guns.

Gun violence is an ongoing issue and the factors controlling it are constantly changing. One of these factors is new laws banning semiautomatic weapons. Another factor is new technology that may give people more protection from gun attacks. With a topic that is forever changing, it is important to keep up to date on laws, rules, and opinions.

NOBODY NEEDS AN AR-15

Not in America Not in Canada!

FALSE CLAIMS

As you gather information, you may find facts that don't line up with what you already know or believe to be true. Without checking facts carefully, people will pass on this information as accurate. Other people will read it and assume it can be trusted. This is how **myths**, lies, and false data spread. Once many people repeat them as true, it may be difficult to challenge them. Checking sources is vital for ensuring accurate information. Look to see who has reported the facts. Remember that individuals or groups will slant facts to fit their bias.

CONSIDER ALL VIEWPOINTS

One way to get a balanced view is to look at a topic from many different perspectives. Different sides in the gun violence debate include gun rights lobbyists, gun control groups, government committees, victims of gun violence, police, and hunters. You can also get a balanced view by understanding the effects on different groups. Gun violence affects everyone from children in schools to government officials.

◄ AR-15s are a type of semiautomatic rifle, which means it self-loads a new round of ammunition into the chamber after shooting. It has been used in many mass shootings in the United States.

WHAT'S AT STAKE?

LOW RISK HIGH RISK

Has access to the Internet helped or hindered our knowledge of gun violence? What are the positives about the wealth of information on the Internet? What are the negatives?

GUNS AND FAMILIES

Gun violence continues to be a problem in many communities. A *Preventive Medicine* study in 2016 shows that 99.85 percent of Americans will know a victim of gun violence in their lifetime. As people demand action to reduce gun violence, communities often respond by putting more police officers on the streets. Statistics show that sheer numbers of police don't make a huge difference, but targeted programs do. New York City has reduced its crime rate and gun violence to record lows through community policing programs that aim to get guns off the streets. The city had a 50 percent reduction in gun injuries in East New York from 2014–2016. Much of this has been attributed to the Cure Violence program. The program targets violence as a public health problem—in other words, like a disease that harms victims, witnesses, and perpetrators. Under the Cure Violence program, shootings, murders, arrests, and instances of officers firing their weapons decreased.

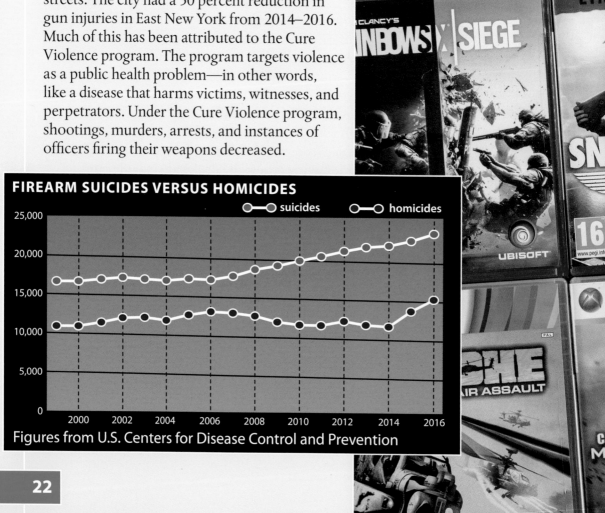

FIREARM SUICIDES VERSUS HOMICIDES

○—○ suicides   ○—○ homicides

Figures from U.S. Centers for Disease Control and Prevention

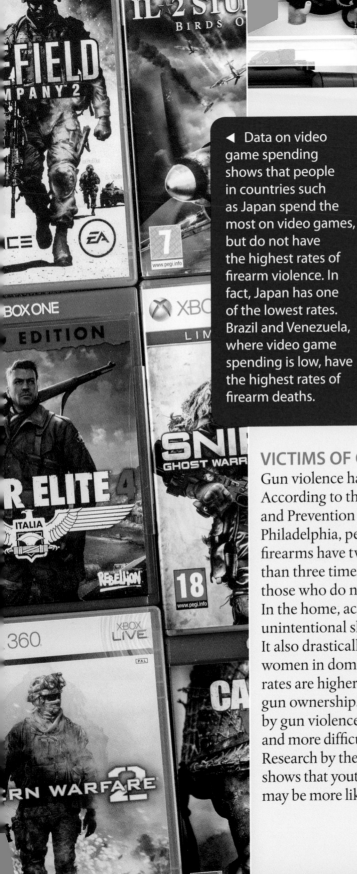

◄ Data on video game spending shows that people in countries such as Japan spend the most on video games, but do not have the highest rates of firearm violence. In fact, Japan has one of the lowest rates. Brazil and Venezuela, where video game spending is low, have the highest rates of firearm deaths.

WHAT'S AT STAKE?

Do you think that children who watch movies containing a lot of guns and gun violence are more likely to handle and want to shoot guns? Why or why not? What do you think parents, guardians, and teachers can or should do to minimize the risk of children accepting gun violence as normal?

VICTIMS OF GUN VIOLENCE

Gun violence has a huge effect on families too. According to the Center for Injury Research and Prevention at the Children's Hospital of Philadelphia, people who report having access to firearms have twice the risk of homicide, and more than three times the risk of suicide compared to those who do not own or have access to firearms. In the home, access to a gun increases the risk of unintentional shooting deaths among children. It also drastically increases the risk of death for women in domestic violence situations. Suicide rates are higher in states that have higher rates of gun ownership. Studies also show children affected by gun violence have higher incidences of **anxiety**, and more difficulty sleeping and concentrating. Research by the National Institute on Drug Abuse shows that youth who are exposed to gun violence may be more likely to join violent gangs.

Gun violence can also worsen existing problems in society. **Racism** creates targets for hate. FBI data shows that while hate crimes against **minorities**, including acts using guns, have been going down, incidents against blacks, **Muslims**, and Jews are on the rise again.

In early U.S. history, slave owners were allowed to own guns, but slaves were not. During the Civil War (1861–1865), blacks who served in the army were allowed guns. However, after the Civil War ended, laws called the Black Codes were passed. White lawmakers worried that black Americans, angry at how they were still being treated, would rise up against those in power. The laws they passed removed many rights of black Americans, including banning them from having guns.

FEELING THREATENED

Today, many minorities worry that gun laws will reflect racist attitudes that view people of color who own guns as a threat—instead of **law-abiding** citizens who have a legal right to them. Statistics from the Centers for Disease Control and Prevention, a national health-monitoring agency in the United States, show that black Americans are eight times more likely to be killed by guns than those who are white. These same statistics show that black men who live in urban areas are more likely to be victims of homicide than those in rural areas. There are different homicide rates between states too. States, such as Wisconsin, that have big gaps in advantages between white and black Americans—such as employment opportunities—also tend to have more gun violence victims along racial lines. Out of all homicides for black victims, the weapon used in 86 percent of the deaths was a gun.

KEY PLAYERS

The National African-American Gun Association was founded in 2015. It is a group that believes African Americans need guns to protect themselves and that gun control laws will make them more **vulnerable**. It promotes the idea of safe gun use for African Americans who own guns for protection, shooting competitions, and outdoor activities.

JAIL for Zimmerman

A MOVEMENT JUSTICE FOR TRAYVONS

▶ These marchers are protesting gun violence against black Americans. Seventeen-year-old Trayvon Martin was shot by George Zimmerman on February 26, 2012, in Sanford, Florida. Like 70 percent of black homicide victims, Trayvon was not committing a crime when he was shot. He was visiting relatives and was unarmed. Zimmerman claimed he shot Trayvon in self-defense.

> "Saying gun laws are always racist is just false. Saying that gun laws have never been racist is also just wrong.
>
> Saul Cornell, American history professor, Fordham University

Students spend anywhere from 800 to 1,000 hours in school each year. But schools, colleges, and universities have also become targets for mass shootings and gun violence. That means the place where students spend most of their time is becoming a place of fear. Schools have tried to create a safe space with **lockdown** drills, metal detectors, and security. This has done very little to stop the gun violence that is still happening in schools, especially in the United States.

Almost all schools deal with issues of bullying, hatred, and **discrimination**. Students get angry or feel threatened. If they have access to guns and can get them into the buildings, it can lead to tragedy. There are problems with the safety

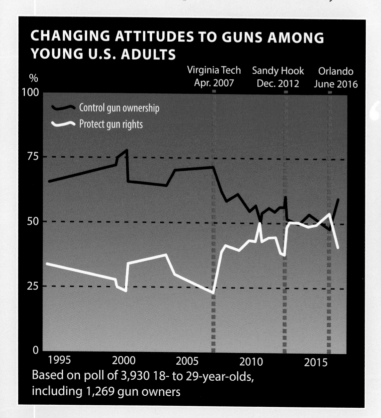

CHANGING ATTITUDES TO GUNS AMONG YOUNG U.S. ADULTS

Virginia Tech
Apr. 2007

Sandy Hook
Dec. 2012

Orlando
June 2016

— Control gun ownership
— Protect gun rights

Based on poll of 3,930 18- to 29-year-olds, including 1,269 gun owners

> "Attending a high school where a homicide takes place prompts trauma, and that impacts students' school experience and achievement."
>
> Daniel Willingham, psychology professor, University of Virginia

features in schools. Not all schools have metal detectors. Those that do may not use them every day. Security guards need to take breaks or might lose concentration. This leaves gaps that attackers can take advantage of.

NO TIME TO REACT

Statistics show that many school shootings are personal, between just two or three people. These shootings are targeted and are over in only a few seconds. Teachers, security, and police have no time to stop them. Students in schools with gun violence suffer emotional damage that lasts long after the event. A study in *Pediatrics* showed that it didn't matter if the student was a direct victim of the attack or just a witness. The resulting **trauma** was almost the same.

Mass shootings, such as those at Columbine, Sandy Hook, or Marjory Stoneman Douglas, make national news. These school shootings have motivated students to protest gun laws. These young people feel that adults are not doing enough to protect them. Marches, speeches, and rallies demand change from the government.

◄ Miami police take part in an active shooter drill at the beginning of a new school year. Lockdown and "Run, Hide, Fight" drills are now a part of many schools' routines.

◄ In 2018, students were at the forefront of demonstrations demanding new gun laws. They feel more needs to be done to protect them.

ASK YOUR OWN QUESTIONS

Do teachers pay enough attention to mental health issues? How likely are students to report a classmate's strange behavior or threats? Should **social media** accounts be monitored for danger signs?

In the United States and Canada, the right to assemble at public events and places is guaranteed. Concerts, football games, protests, festivals—these are all places where we can get together, celebrate, or make our voices heard. Gun violence has **impacted** and changed how we gather in numbers. In a 2017 Gallup poll, 38 percent of U.S. adults said they were less willing to attend events with large crowds. Security has also become tighter at concerts. Teams work with venue staff to map exits for performers and fans. Organizations such as the Onsite Foundation in Nashville provide funding for victims of mass shootings to give them access to trauma therapy.

ON HIGH ALERT

The deadly attack at an outdoor Las Vegas concert in October 2017 (see page 18) changed the way these events are planned and run. Drones are now used to watch from the skies. Security staff are trained to spot anything that looks out of place, like a garbage can that has been moved or a person not watching the event. These new security measures cost a lot of money. Most big events now spend many thousands of dollars on security. This means ticket costs have to go up.

Hotel security experts, such as Todd Seiders of Petra Risk Solutions in California, say they are not even sure that they can prevent such tragedies in the future. They argue that the Las Vegas hotel where the shooter booked a room already had good security. The question after the shooting was whether or not people would still attend these events. It seems that people are happy being delayed or spending more money for better security because they don't want to give up going to events, traveling, or joining in protests.

WHAT'S AT STAKE?

LOW RISK HIGH RISK

Security at public events and spaces can be very **invasive** and not always successful at preventing tragedy. How far is too far in terms of giving up your privacy in exchange for protection?

▶ It is difficult for police to patrol all public places where there are a lot of people every day, such as downtown or tourist areas, and at train and bus stations.

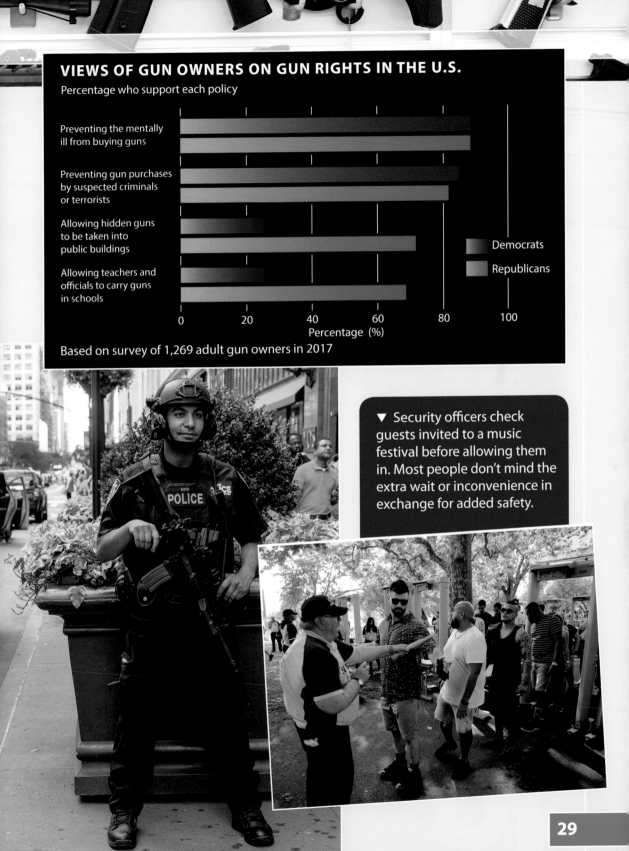

VIEWS OF GUN OWNERS ON GUN RIGHTS IN THE U.S.

Percentage who support each policy

Preventing the mentally ill from buying guns

Preventing gun purchases by suspected criminals or terrorists

Allowing hidden guns to be taken into public buildings

Allowing teachers and officials to carry guns in schools

Democrats
Republicans

0   20   40   60   80   100
Percentage (%)

Based on survey of 1,269 adult gun owners in 2017

▼ Security officers check guests invited to a music festival before allowing them in. Most people don't mind the extra wait or inconvenience in exchange for added safety.

Guns and gun violence are not going away anytime soon. In the United States, statistics show that while violent crime is decreasing, gun deaths overall are not. Shootings have increased and more guns are getting into the hands of the wrong people. While in most states you do not need a permit to buy a gun, legal gun dealers do background checks on gun buyers. People who sell only a few guns from a private collection are not considered dealers. They can sell privately to whomever they want. This is one way guns can be sold to people with mental illness or a criminal past.

Get **$1,000** Cash reward for your information that leads to a person with an illegal gun.

NO Name ID Questions

Reciba una recompensa de **$1,000** por su información que conduzca a una persona con un arma ilegal.

NO Nombre Identificación Preguntas

Call

THE CENTRAL ISSUES

What plays the biggest role in controlling and decreasing gun violence? Is it, for example, gun control, gun laws, cracking down on gangs, or ending poverty? Find reliable studies with statistics that support your answer.

> "As for gun control advocates, I have no hope whatever that any facts whatever will make the slightest dent in their thinking — or lack of thinking."
>
> Thomas Sowell,
> U.S. economist and social theorist

◄ This billboard in Miami, Florida advertises a program that pays people for reporting illegal guns. The hope is that the reward will encourage people to help them get some guns off the streets.

3-D PRINTED WEAPONS

New technology may be creating a new way for dangerous people to get their hands on a gun. 3-D printers are able to print guns. In 2013, Defense Distributed, a gun-rights **activist** organization provided free online blueprints for a 3-D printed gun. The guns are not ready to use—metal parts are needed for the firing pin—but instructions are given on how to complete them.

Many people are worried because these guns are **untraceable**. That means they can be used in a crime and the police have no way of finding who owned them. There are also no background checks, so anyone can download the instructions and get a gun. Because they are made of plastic, they are also easier to destroy after a crime than a metal gun. When the plans came online, 19 U.S. states filed a lawsuit to block them. The state authorities are worried about public safety.

ACROSS THE BORDER

Even though Canada has tougher gun control laws, gun violence there is increasing. In the country's large cities, police say most killings are linked to gangs. Many guns used in crimes are smuggled into Canada across the border from the United States, where they are easily bought. Other guns are stolen from legal owners. While Americans can legally manufacture firearms for their own use, it is illegal in Canada. Fewer 3-D guns are likely to be printed in Canada because Canadians can face prison time for doing so. Criminals, though, rarely worry about gun control laws and regulations.

SEARCH TIPS

To find an expert doing current research on a topic such as U.S. and Canadian gun laws, use these search tools. Type the subject into each search bar.

Google Scholar: https://scholar.google.ca

Microsoft Academic: https://academic.microsoft.com

Expertise Finder: http://expertisefinder.com

The largest gun-rights group in the United States is the National Rifle Association of America (NRA). It was set up in 1871 to promote marksmanship. In the 1970s, it officially began trying to persuade lawmakers to alter and block gun legislation.

Like most lobby groups, the NRA does this by contributing money and assistance to members of **Congress**. The money helps politicians mount election campaigns and stay in office. Gun-rights groups, such as the NRA, outspend groups from the opposite position. Critics say this is unfair because politicians receiving a lot of money from the NRA are more likely to support its agenda instead of one that reflects the stricter gun laws. The NRA represents close to six million members across the United States. It opposes laws that restrict people's rights to buy, own, or use firearms. The NRA believes the way to fight gun violence is for more people to be armed.

STARTING A MOVEMENT

When a former student entered Marjory Stoneman Douglas High School in Parkland, Florida, on February 14, 2018, he killed 17 students and teachers and wounded 17 more. The survivors started the Never Again Movement. They wanted to force change in gun control laws. They organized the March for Our Lives rallies across the United States. An NRA spokesman said that the students were marching for less freedom.

The NRA has become a target of the Parkland students who think it has too much power to determine laws about gun control. Many of the students are now becoming old enough to vote as adult citizens. The Never Again Movement is working to make sure all eligible students are registered and get out and vote.

▶ In the United States, there are nearly six times the number of gun stores as Starbucks coffee shops. These stores must have a Federal Firearms License and keep careful records of stock and sales.

▲ A concealed carry permit means the gun owner can legally carry their gun even though it can't be seen. As of 2018, there were more than 17 million concealed carry permits given out in the United States.

CLASH OF BELIEFS

On July 22, 2018, a gunman opened fire in the Greektown area of Toronto on Danforth Avenue. He killed two people and wounded 13 before killing himself. The gun used was illegal. It was bought from gang sources and reportedly came from the United States. In the past, most illegal guns came across the border, but that is not always the case now. Detective Di Danieli of the guns and gangs unit of the Toronto Police Service said more and more guns used for criminal activity are being bought from legal gun owners who sell them for profit.

Mass shootings happen often in America—on average, there is a mass shooting nine out of every ten days. They have become more frequent in the last two decades. Mass shootings are shocking and tragic and they grab our attention. Yet most gun violence in the country isn't the result of a mass shooting. According to statistics, two-thirds of the gun deaths each year in the country are suicides. Mental health advocates say many of these deaths could be prevented with better mental health awareness and care. Statistics also show that programs that target and reduce some of the contributing factors to gun violence, such as crime and easy access to weapons, can cut down on everyday gun violence.

GUN RELATIONSHIPS

Our relationship to guns influences how we view gun policy or the course of action and laws taken by our governments. It also influences how we feel when confronted with opposing views about gun use and abuse. The histories of some countries are more closely linked to gun use and the freedom to own and use guns. The link between access to guns and gun violence is also clear. Globally, the United States has the most guns per person. According to the Graduate Institute of International and Development Studies in Geneva, there are more than 120 guns for every 100 people in the United States.

FIREARMS LAWS

Evidence from countries around the world shows tighter gun legislation results in fewer incidents of gun violence. Legislation includes requiring background checks, gun certificates, safety training, registration, and licenses as is done in Canada, the United Kingdom, and Japan. These countries have kept gun violence lower than the United States. Keeping strict control over who can buy and use a gun does help keep guns out of the hands of criminals. Less easy access to a gun may also prevent shooting in anger.

WHAT'S AT STAKE?

How important is it to be open-minded when researching a topic? Why will some people try to stop you from questioning popular ideas? Can you always convince others of the truth? Why or why not?

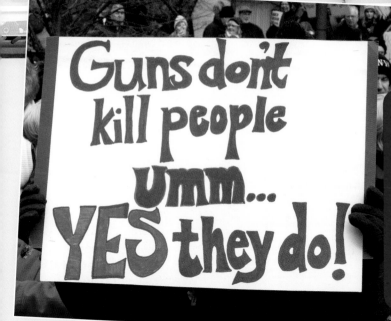

◄ "Guns don't kill people, people kill people" is a common saying used when acts of gun violence occur. While it is true that people make the decision to use guns in violent acts, the U.S. has a seven percent higher rate of murders using guns compared to countries with stricter gun laws.

◄ Pro-gun supporters gather outside an NRA convention. They carry their guns in the open to support their belief that more guns do not lead to more gun violence.

> There is no reason why anyone needs to own a device that can fire 90 bullets every 10 seconds but for the mass killing of people.

Dannel Malloy, former governor of Connecticut

Most gun owners in the U.S. believe the right to bear arms is a part of their basic freedoms. Many who don't own guns believe they have a right to be free from gun violence as well. The two groups are often divided on gun policy. Many agree on certain restrictions, such as preventing people with mental illnesses from buying and owning guns.

CANADIAN GUN LAWS

In Canada, gun ownership is controlled. People wanting guns have to prove they are stable, law-abiding, and no danger to society. But there is still gun violence. Each new government voted into power has a different idea of how to regulate guns to limit gun violence. A new law, Bill C-71, will tighten background checks and the recording of gun sales.

Two types of guns would also be banned because they are similar to military-style weapons. The law would permit police to check a person's entire history for criminal or unstable behavior, not just the previous five years.

U.S. GUN CONTROL DEBATE

In the United States, gun control is a very **controversial** topic. The NRA opposes laws that restrict a person's right to buy, have, or use guns. However, a poll released in 2018 by the Quinnipiac University Polling Institute in Connecticut, shows that more than 66 percent of U.S. citizens are in favor of stricter gun control. With each mass shooting, especially in schools, that number seems to rise.

▼ Wayne LaPierre Jr., CEO of the National Rifle Association, is shown on a banner for the NRA's annual convention in 2018. LaPierre has called for schools to increase their security and arm teachers to protect themselves from increased gun violence and mass shootings.

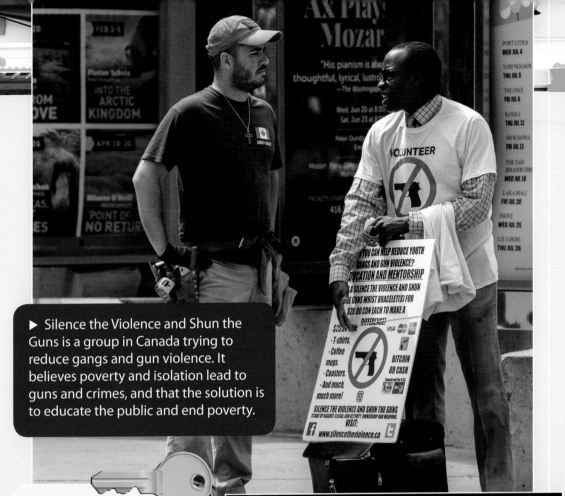

▶ Silence the Violence and Shun the Guns is a group in Canada trying to reduce gangs and gun violence. It believes poverty and isolation lead to guns and crimes, and that the solution is to educate the public and end poverty.

KEY PLAYERS

Canada's **National Firearms Association** was set up in 1978. Similar to the NRA in the United States, it is a nonprofit lobby group that promotes, supports, and protects citizens' gun rights, safe firearms activities, and the right of self-defense. It provides firearms education for all Canadians and freedom and justice for Canada's firearms community.

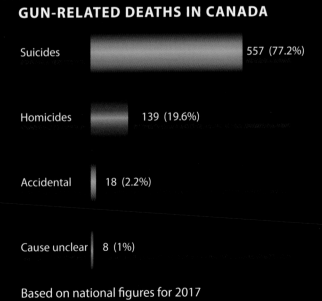

GUN-RELATED DEATHS IN CANADA

Suicides	557 (77.2%)
Homicides	139 (19.6%)
Accidental	18 (2.2%)
Cause unclear	8 (1%)

Based on national figures for 2017

Countries around the world not only have very different levels of gun violence but also gun control. Groups in North America that are in favor of more restrictions, such as who can have guns and what types of guns, look to countries such as Japan, Australia, and the United Kingdom for examples of legislation.

▶ In the UK, firearms are considered dangerous weapons. The police are the licensing authority for firearms.

GUN LAWS IN JAPAN

Even though Japan has about 127 million people, it has an average of only 10 gun deaths each year. Japanese law states that "no person shall possess a firearm or firearms or a sword or swords." Citizens can buy only shotguns and rifles—no handguns—because the only reason you can get a gun is if you are a hunter or for sport shooting at

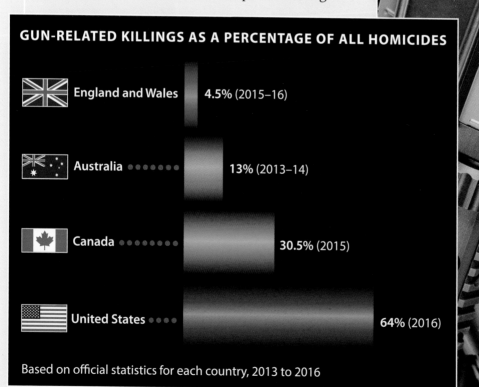

GUN-RELATED KILLINGS AS A PERCENTAGE OF ALL HOMICIDES

England and Wales — 4.5% (2015–16)

Australia — 13% (2013–14)

Canada — 30.5% (2015)

United States — 64% (2016)

Based on official statistics for each country, 2013 to 2016

▲ A display of the illegal guns and weapons seized by police in China in 146 cities across the country. Ordinary citizens are not allowed to own guns except for hunting. Illegally owning guns will result in at least three years in prison or, in serious cases, death.

> " Australia's 1996 gun law reforms were followed by more than a decade free of fatal mass shootings, and accelerated declines in firearm deaths, particularly suicides. "
>
> Article in the journal *Injury Prevention*

a range. Gun owners have to be trained in their use, attend a firearms class, pass a firearms test, have an in-hospital mental health check, and have their background thoroughly checked. Gun owners can also buy more ammunition only by turning in empty **magazines**. Every three years they must retake a firearms class and test.

GUN LAWS IN AUSTRALIA

After the 1996 mass shooting in Port Arthur, Tasmania, the Australian government banned automatic and semiautomatic rifles and shotguns. They also bought back more than 600,000 guns and destroyed them. They started a gun registry and made it harder to get a license. People wanting to buy a gun have to wait 28 days.

At the time, anti-gun control groups in Australia were supported by the U.S.-based NRA in their attempts to stop laws restricting guns for law-abiding citizens. But pro-gun control groups pointed out that most people who committed acts of gun violence did not have a criminal record or known mental health problems. Their access to guns was the reason for homicide and mass-shooting tragedies. After the changes to gun laws, not only has there not been another mass shooting in Australia, but gun homicide and suicide rates have also gone down.

GET INVOLVED

So you've researched the history of gun violence and gun control. You've learned the key vocabulary and key people involved in the issue. You're up to date on gun control laws under debate and the changing homicide, suicide, and mass-shooting rates. What now? Gun violence, like many current topics, is constantly changing. With every election, each new invention, and the next shooting, the issue shifts.

INTERNET SEARCHES

When looking at websites, address extensions can help identify the sources of the information.

.gov (government)— official government organizations or departments. You may not be able to access all areas of these websites.

.org (organization)— usually nonprofit organizations and charities.

.com (commercial)— mostly businesses. It is the most widely used web address extension.

Country extensions:

.ca   Canada
.us   United States
.au   Australia
.uk   United Kingdom
.ru   Russia
.de   Germany

◄ Online news is more current than print news or even scheduled TV news programs. Events and details can be updated as they happen. Online news channels also have live footage of an unfolding event, natural disaster, or press conference.

WHERE TO LOOK NOW

To stay informed about gun violence and actions being taken to reduce it, use sources such as these:

- Online news streaming, for example, *TIME Edge* and *CNN Student News*. For international news, try the BBC. Check evening news programs and documentaries, such as *The Fifth Estate* in Canada or *60 Minutes* in the United States, for segments on gun violence and gun control.
- Newspapers and magazines such as *The New York Times*, *The Washington Post*, and *The Wall Street Journal* in the United States. In Canada, try *The Globe and Mail* and *Maclean's*. For global news, look for *The Times* and *The Guardian* in the UK.
- Websites for organizations on both sides of the issue, for example, Brady Campaign to Prevent Gun Violence, Americans for Gun Safety Foundation, American Hunters and Shooters Association, National Rifle Association, National Firearms Association, and Coalition for Gun Control.
- Experts on gun violence, including law enforcement officers, researchers, data and statistics investigators.
- Google Alerts for new developments or articles about gun violence.
- Podcasts and radio programs dealing with violence and/or gun control such as *Youth Radio*.

Be sure to have a varied and balanced **news diet** and, whichever sources you use, be alert for bias, prejudice, and context. Check any facts with objective statistics and experts on the subject.

Gun violence is an issue that affects all of us. If you do not know how and where to protect yourself from gun violence, you could be putting your life at risk. However, if you listen only to headlines and news stories, you could be so terrified that you are afraid to leave your house. You must get accurate information.

Besides the impact it will have on you personally, getting an accurate view of an issue can give you the tools to make a difference in society. You may be able to educate others about the importance of the issue and add your voice to the discussion. You can bring awareness of the different perspectives on the topic. You will be able to sign petitions or attend rallies with real understanding of why you are supporting one side over the other.

Maybe you will feel inspired to contact your local politicians to make sure they are working for everyone in their area, not just one group or organization. Maybe you will advocate for better education about gun violence. With a good grasp of the issue, you can state your case and defend your ideas with confidence.

SKILLS FOR LIFE

Checking for bias and prejudice surrounding gun violence will make you aware of a balanced view in other topics. You will learn to look at a speech, magazine article, or news report and see or hear the slant someone is putting on it. You will not be easily swayed or convinced by people who have their own **agendas**. You will ask questions and get to the bottom of a topic to the truth. These skills will make you better able to make good decisions for yourself and your society in general.

▼ Students have been one of the biggest voices for change in gun laws. As they become old enough to vote, they will be able to create a government that speaks for them and challenge or support lobby groups such as the NRA as they see fit.

LOW RISK   HIGH RISK

WHAT'S AT STAKE?

What is the price of doing nothing about topics such as gun violence? Can you criticize decision-makers if you don't get involved?

ANNUAL SPENDING ON LOBBYING AGAINST GUN CONTROL BY NRA

Millions of dollars ($)

4

3

2

1

0

2008 2009 2010 2011 2012 2013 2014 2015 2016 2017

Based on figures from U.S. National Rifle Association

INTERNET SEARCH TIPS

- Use quotation marks around a phrase to search for that exact combination of words (for example, "mass shootings").
- Use the minus sign to eliminate certain words from your search (for example, gun violence – suicide).
- Use a colon and an extension to search a specific site (for example, semiautomatic weapons:.gov for all government website mentions of that particular gun).
- Use the word Define and a colon to search for word definitions (for example, Define: homicide).

GLOSSARY

action groups Groups that try to bring about change, usually by discussion but sometimes by force

activist A person who campaigns to bring about social change

agendas Underlying plans

analyze To study or look at in detail, thoroughly

anxiety A feeling of worry

assassinate To kill someone, such as a famous or important person, usually for political reasons

background check An official investigation into someone's personal history for possible criminal activity

civil rights People's rights for equal treatment and equal opportunities

clickbait An online encouragement to read or hear something

communities Collections of people who live in an area

compiled Information collected and sorted into a list or report

Congress The group of people who are responsible for making the laws of a counry

constitution The set of rules used to govern an organization or country

context Circumstances, background, or setting for an event, idea, or activity

controversial A topic that is argued over

corrupt Act dishonestly in return for money

credible Able to be trusted or believed

criminals People who break laws

databases Organized collections of information

debate A discussion where all sides and perspectives of a topic are considered

dependable Reliable

disarmed Took weapons away

discrimination Treating one person or group in a worse way based on their looks, religion, or ideas

evidence Facts or information that prove if something is true or real

factors Things that help influence a result

firearms Anything that can shoot, in particular guns, rifles, shotguns

homicide Killing another person

impacted Strongly affected

interpretations Explanations of the meaning of something

invasive Spreading in a harmful way

key Main, most important

law-abiding Obeying the rules

lobby groups Groups that try to influence laws and decisions of politicians

lockdown Security measure involving closing and locking doors to prevent people entering

magazines Chambers for holding ammunition in guns

media Mass communications such as radio, TV, books, the Internet

minorities Small groups of people who are similar within a larger group

mission An objective to change something

mobilize Move into action

Muslims People who belong to the religion of Islam

myths False beliefs or ideas that people hold true

news diet The sources you use to get your news

objective Not taking sides

perspective Viewpoint

politicians Citizens' representatives that serve in government

prejudices Opinions not based on reason

privileges Special rights or advantages

racial tension Hostile act by one racial group toward another

racism Prejudice or hatred directed at another race

registry A record or list of something

smuggle Move things illegally in or out of a country

social media Websites and computer software that let people communicate and share information

society People living and working together in a country in an organized way

source material Any collection of information that can be studied to get informed and stay informed

statistics A type of math that deals with the collection, analysis, and presentation of numerical data

swayed Easily influenced

tragedy A very sad event

trauma A deeply distressing experience

untraceable Not able to find or follow something

victim A person who has been harmed, attacked, or injured by someone else

violation A break of the rules or laws

vulnerable Able to be easily controlled or influenced

SOURCE NOTES

QUOTATIONS

p. 4: Warren, Elizabeth. *A Fighting Chance*. Metropolitan Books, 2014.

p. 11: https://www.thetrace.org/2016/08/hillary-clinton-quotes-on-guns/

p. 15: https://dailym.ai/2NFcjyt

p. 18: https://abcn.ws/2pRsO12

p. 21: http://politicalticker.blogs.cnn.com/category/sam-brownback/page/5/
https://bit.ly/2pVLaOw

p. 25: https://bit.ly/2yjhIGD

p. 26: https://bit.ly/2pVPrS5

p. 31: https://www.creators.com/read/thomas-sowell/07/12/news-versus-propaganda

p. 35: https://www.cnn.com/2018/04/09/us/gun-laws-since-parkland/index.html

p. 39: https://www.ncbi.nlm.nih.gov/pmc/articles/PMC2704353/

REFERENCES USED FOR THIS BOOK

Chapter 1: The Need to Know, pp. 4–7
https://www.macleans.ca/opinion/gun-violence-isnt-just-a-u-s-problem-and-canada-isnt-immune/
https://bit.ly/2yjIL4N
https://www.gunviolencearchive.org

Chapter 2: How to Get Informed, pp. 8–13
https://westernreservepublicmedia.org/history
analyze.htm
https://www.ojjdp.gov/pubs/gun_violence/sect01.html

Chapter 3: How Did We Get Here?, pp. 14–19
https://theconversation.com/u-s-gun-violence-is-a-symptom-of-a-long-historical-problem-92322
https://www.globalresearch.ca
http://www.rcmp-grc.gc.ca/cfp-pcaf/pol-leg/hist/con-eng.htm
https://www.history.com/topics/1990s/columbine-high-school-shootings

Chapter 4: Information Literacy, pp. 20–29
https://www.cwla.org/the-impact-of-gun-violence-on-children-families-communities/
https://wapo.st/2OWXhJi
https://tinyurl.com/ybgdj75k
https://read.bi/2OrSiAW
https://bit.ly/2Q9wMky
https://tinyurl.com/y884bsww
https://www.acpm.org/page/preventivemedicine

Chapter 5: Recent Developments, pp. 30–39
https://www.cnet.com/news/the-3d-printed-gun-controversy-everything-you-need-to-know/
https://bit.ly/2EDOiEk
https://bit.ly/2AcMuT0
https://read.bi/2RHZeaX
https://bit.ly/2xaquZ4

Chapter 6: Get Involved, pp. 40-43
https://bit.ly/2pT9L6o
https://bit.ly/2yEtV6P
https://twitter.com/Emma4Change
https://twitter.com/davidhogg111

FIND OUT MORE

Finding good source material on the Internet can sometimes be a challenge. When analyzing how reliable the information is, consider these points:

- Who is the author of the page? Is it an expert in the field or a person who experienced the event?

- Is the site well known and up to date? A page that has not been updated for several years probably has out-of-date information.

- Can you verify the facts with another site? Always double-check information.

- Have you checked all possible sites? Don't just look on the first page a search engine provides.

- Remember to try government sites and research papers.

- Have you recorded website addresses and names? Keep this data so you can backtrack later and verify the information you want to use.

WEBSITES

Find up-to-date statistics on gun violence.
https://www.gunviolencearchive.org

Gun safety for kids from KidsHealth.
https://kidshealth.org/en/kids/gun-safety.html

Keep informed on the March for Our Lives Movement.
https://marchforourlives.com

Learn about your right to vote with Everytown for Gun Safety.
https://everytown.org

BOOKS

Braden, Ann. *The Benefits of Being an Octopus*. Sky Pony Press, 2018.

Going, K. L. *Pieces of Why*. Kathy Dawson Books, 2015.

Moore, David Barclay. *The Stars Beneath Our Feet*. Knopf Books for Young Readers, 2017.

Reynolds, Jason. *Long Way Down*. Atheneum, 2017.

ABOUT THE AUTHOR

Natalie Hyde has written more than 75 fiction and nonfiction books for kids. She shares her home with a little leopard gecko and a cat that desperately wants to eat it.

INDEX